SPEAK!
The Project

SeLisa Godfrey

SPEAK! The Project

Copyright © 2019 SeLisa Godfrey

All rights reserved. No portion of this book may be reproduced, stored in a retrieval system, or transmitted in any form or by any means—electronic, mechanical, photocopy, recording, scanning, or other—except for brief quotations in critical reviews or articles, without the prior written permission of the publisher.

Cover Design: Alyssa Banks at The SanctiFly Brand.

Cover Photo: Joel Sutton at Joel Onais Photography

Scriptures marked KJV are taken from the KING JAMES VERSION (KJV): KING JAMES VERSION, public domain.

Scriptures marked NLT are taken from the HOLY BIBLE, NEW LIVING TRANSLATION (NLT): Scriptures taken from the HOLY BIBLE, NEW LIVING TRANSLATION, Copyright© 1996, 2004, 2007 by Tyndale House Foundation. Used by permission of Tyndale House Publishers, Inc., Carol Stream, Illinois 60188. All rights reserved. Used by permission.

Godfrey, SeLisa. Speak! The Project.

ISBN: 978-0-578-57344-1

Dedication

To Pastor Glenn Sawyer for planting the idea in me and waiting for it to come into fruition.

To David: For many years, you were my Muse, and in some ways, you still are!

And to the wonderful memory of great, supportive friends who were unable to see the vision come to pass, John E. Sutton, Mark Weaver, and James Perry. Forever in my heart!

Table of Contents

Dedication i

Acknowledgements iv

4-Letter Word 1

The One 3

If Home is Where the Heart Is
    Part 1 7
    Part 2 8

Someone 12

Has Been 14

He Wanted to Die 19

Conversation 23

Breathe 26

Transfusion 29

A Heart That Forgives 33

Garden Eviction 36

I'm Just Tired 40

Today I Cried 42

Stages 43

I Cry (A Black History Poem) 46

A Mother's Day Tribute 49

Dear Dad 52

I'm a Raisin (Raising) 54

Bonus: Dearest Pastor 57

Acknowledgements

I'm grateful to *God* first and foremost for enabling me to write in this magnitude. Thank you, Lord, that through your son Jesus, you saved me from my sins, myself, and the wreck. I honestly believe my life has meaning.

To my editors Roderick Evans & Ganelle Sutton. Thank you for helping me to bring this project into fruition.

To my Mom, for always being my biggest supporter and encourager, and my Dad for helping whenever possible. Love you both. To CJ, my not so little brother, I look up to you in more ways than one, and to my SIL-E, Faith, thanks for adding value to our family. An extra special shout out to my uncle, Carlton Sutton, Sr. for believing in this project long before it was a project. You've always been everything our family has needed. And to all my other aunts, uncles, and cousins on both sides (Sutton, Bailey, Godfrey, Murden) for your continued prayers, support, and encouragement!

My sisterly friends; Kellie, Katina, Alyssa, Kim, Valerie, J. Noel (Henderson), and Kaysha: thanks for your constant and consistent prayers and reminding me to look at the big picture. Also, to my BFF Jill, Best Fran (again), and Joel Sutton for your direct help on this project!

To Connie Sawyer III and Kevin "KD" Dixon for your legal advice and support! To Marsharel, Kelvin, Anthony, and Elbert for your listening ear and honest critiques. Love you guys! And to the one who wishes to remain anonymous, thank you for the years of feedback. As well as Sully. Whenever or however I needed you for whatever phase of my life, you were there. For the one millionth and third time, thank you and I love you.

To the Blounts, Pennys, Boones, Browns, and Perrymans, my vocal supporters; I love and appreciate you! To my bros Abel Sutton, Michael Sutton, and Javaris Jones. You don't just speak encouragement, you live it, and I couldn't have pulled it off without you! I love you and your family, and I pray that God bless and keep you all!

My church family, New Mt. Zion COGIC Deliverance Center, Pastor Glenn Sawyer, and Lady Sandra Sawyer, love you all and thanks for your support.

To every person (especially my former colleagues at CMS, HLT, and CHS), school, and church that allowed me to speak to your group or people, or even yourself, thank you.

4-Letter Word

Many of us in Christendom find ourselves lusting after the flesh rather than the Spirit. This first poem takes the position of a person who realizes that first, I'm sinning. Second, I don't want to. And third, Christ is the solution to my problem.

Friday, August 6, 2010

Love is a verb.
It's an action word.
And that's what I thought I had for you,
But that can't be true.
Yes, yesterday's actions did spell that 4-letter word,
But it was L-U-S-T
Not L-O-V-E!
Can't you see, that was never meant to be?
It's not part of a better plan;
That was just man being man.
I love HIM,
But that's not what I told HIM
When I closed my eyes
and you started to rise
above me to love me.
My bad…lust me!
Trust me I wanted it too,
But true love doesn't do what it feels.
It yields its will to the Lord
Because we can't afford
Not to do it right.
Our relationship is too precious for that.
No measure of that
can enter in.
That leads us to sin, and sin just can win.

I know I said it before and now I'm sayin' it again:
Our best interest is to let our interest
Be overtaken by Christ.
He's the only right
I know that can make sure we take it slow
And not go back to lusting
But trusting that our actions are true.
That I act like
I LOVE YOU!

The One

I fell in love my freshman year of high school. I know people say you're too young to know what love is and it's just puppy love, but I really was in love. The problem was, I constantly struggled with loving who he was going to be (figuring one day he would be "the one") and being content with the love Christ gave me as The One. Here's a glimpse into that struggle.

Aug/Sept. 2010

They saw:
"Wise beyond her years,"
But never could see the tears
That streamed down my face,
Begging for grace.
There wasn't enough wisdom to keep me in the race.
Yes, I once chased
Like Elmer Fudd after that silly rabbit.
I won't forget it.
HE was so special to me.
HIS love for me exceeded any love I had ever known before.
HE spoke <u>ALL </u>the right words revealing what was in store for "us."
Yes, "us" was a must and I fought to keep what we had.
This ONE was the ONE
That very special man!
HE clothed me in the most flyest garments of love.
Left the most beautiful fragrances outside of my window in the form of flowers.
HE'd talk to me for hours on end.
This ONE, the ONE, was my Best Friend!
So then comes this man, HIS man,
My new friend
That HE gave to me,

Molded for me,
Wanted for me,
Or at least that's what I said to me.
For you see he almost led me from
The ONE who held me in HIS hands.
He talked righteously
But acted differently around me.
This brother wanted to greet with a "Holy" kiss
But didn't want to turn Ms. Into Mrs.
He thought his ministry included touching me
And some things that happened I'll never forget it.
As a matter of fact, I regret it!
But I mean that's what was supposed to happen, right?
This wasn't quite the way I thought it should go,
But I figured with time he'd grow
And stop trying to put the cart before the horse.
But he didn't, of course.
And with every apology he gave to me
I forgave him, you see,
And admitted that I wanted it too,
And suggested we start anew
And do it right this time.
But our c.d. must've been on repeat
Because the cycle continued
I was just being used
Over and over and over again.
There was nothing left to give,
Because I'd given it all to him.
The one I believed the ONE had given to me.
HE'd only spoken friendship
But relationship is what we made,
Both too afraid to commit
Because we knew

HE wouldn't keep us under these conditions.
We hadn't even kept ourselves.
So now I'm alone and bound for Hell
And I can't tell anyone
Because remember, I'm "wise beyond my years."
That meant I should have avoided tears
From hurtful situations.
Not realizing there's a whole nation of people
Just like me in the spirit realm.
We just want to touch the hem of the ONE's garment and be made whole.
To be consoled and forgiven
And given a chance to engage in righteous living.
So now, I'm depressed, distressed, there's no rest
Because I have nothing left to give to the ONE who has given so much for me.
So I cry out to HIM, "I have nothing left to give!
Save me from myself, or myself will end
All of me!"
And you know what?
HE did!
HE changed my heart and mind
To reflect HIS love for me.
So now I wait patiently on HIM
And not for him.
I mean, one day he MAY come.
But I wait in expectation for the ONE who I know *is* coming!
For True Love doesn't wait for the right man to come,
But it waits on the ONE who's
Here,
Been here
All our lives.
Realize HIS love,

The ONE
Who died for me,
Died for you.
Chase him too.
For the grace
I was begging for
Has provided a door
That has given us access to the ONE
Who will always
Be down for you!

If Home Is Where the Heart Is

Many of us in our quest for finding love give our hearts away. If the phrase is true then our home or residence is with someone else. This poem follows someone establishing their home, being evicted, meeting Christ and finally giving their heart to Him
.

Part 1
Friday, June 4, 2004

If home is where the heart is
Then mine must be at 1909,
Cause that's where you are
Every time…

I come looking for you
To talk or just to see
The smile on your face
As you're staring at me…

With thoughts racing
Through your complicated mind.
Yet, I still understand you
Because we're two of a kind.

And your home is
Where my heart used to be,
Because I keep your heart
Inside of me!

Part 2
Wednesday, March 6, 2013

If home is where the heart is
Then I must be homeless
Because it seems hopeless
For me to find residence anywhere.
My stability was taken from me
The moment you evicted me
From your life
by trying to make "Ms. Wrong" be right
by turning your house into a home for her
not realizing you can't turn a trick into a treat
and you can't make tough meat tender.
Don't worry I've surrendered my keys
as unnecessary as it may be
since you changed the locks.
I flock from shelter to shelter just so I can
weather the storms of uncertainty
even though I know certainly
you'll never bend on your decision.
I go from soup kitchen to kitchen
Looking for the warmth your embrace once offered
Finding temporary solace but no real comfort.
Tattered and ragged I drag myself to church
Not to search but hoping to be found.
I hang around for some unapparent reason.
I guess it's the season for crying, "Sanctuary."
Will anyone hear my desperate plea?
I'm just lonely, not diseased but yet in need of some spiritual healing

'Cause I still feel him inside of me.
And just as clearly it's as if Jesus speaks
I hear,

"Come unto Me all ye who labor and are heavy laden,
For I've loved you with an everlasting love.
It's called agape in the Greek.
Yep, I'm meek and lowly too
And I'll come after you
Leaving the 99 for the one
who my desire is towards.
Check Solomon 7:10.
Read it again,
Because it's there you will find that you were mine all along.
Reread Jeremiah 3:1-4.
I told you before I don't take my vows lightly;
I'm married to you and I don't practice divorce!
If you read the last line, I brought you to Zion
To live with me forever.
I am your daily bread.
So you don't have to beg
Because I supply your EVERY need according to My riches in glory.
Your load I'll bear,
But you'll have to carry mine.
Trust Me, it'll be fine
since My yoke is easy and burden's light.
I know you cried all last night
But wake up because joy is here!
I'm always near since I promised never to leave you nor forsake you.
I don't know what more I can do
To prove my love to you.

I sacrificed all of Me
When I hung on that tree
Just to show how much I love you.
I gave My life proving Me to be
A friend for life.
Yes the church is my wife
And you can be my bride if you'd just give Me your all.
Be there when I call
And listen when I speak.
Yeah, I want to rule you and be King of our castle
but trust Me I won't hassle you like that last brother
Because I'm the GREATEST brother that ever was.
All I ask is that you let me make your heart My home.
I promise you'll never have to roam
Again because I've prepared a mansion just for You!
But only if you give Me all of thee!
Choose ye this day whom you will serve:
Him or Me?
I stand patiently knocking at the door of your heart!
Let Me in and I'll free you from the sin
That's left you alone and destitute.
I'll give you a positive outlook
But you must decide."

I listened intently
To all He said to me
And it boiled down to a choice:
Beauty or ashes?
Oil of joy or mourning?
Garment of praise or spirit of heaviness? [1]

---

[1] Isaiah 61:3

So with hands raised and heart full of praise
I choose Christ!
And now my home is in heaven
For I've set my affection on things above [2]
Now that my heart's full of Christ's love!

---

[2] Colossians 3:2

Someone

Growing up in church, you often hear testimonies of people who were not interested in their spouse upon their initial meeting. So, when you hear such stories, you try not to count anyone out as a potential. But at some point, you realize a good man isn't good enough if he's not a God man.

Sunday, March 30, 2015

It's evident you're a good man!
You have your head on straight.
You're going in the right direction
as you try to navigate
through this journey called life.
You made it through misfortunes, mishaps, and strife.
And even though you seem so right,
I know it's want talking and not need
because someone like me needs
Someone who can intercede
and go to God on my behalf,
not just make me laugh or chuckle.
Someone like me needs
Someone who reads the Bible
more than he does the latest Facebook status or Instagram post.
He has a clear understanding of what matters most
and that's having a relationship with Christ.
Someone like me needs
Someone who doesn't just want to do right.
He does right.
When he makes mistakes or errors,
as humans do,
he quickly tries to correct it

because he's Christian too,
and he knows Christ would want him to.
Someone like me needs
Someone like Him!
Not the man constantly taking selfies in the mirror
but the man who reflects Christ
in the way he lives,
the way he gives.
Someone who will love me
like Christ loves the church;
a self-sacrificing love never intentionally hurts
but helps and heals.
Someone like me needs
Someone who is willing to share,
willing to care.
May sometimes fear,
but doesn't let fear control his life
Since 2 Timothy 1:7 told him it's not a gift from Heaven.
Someone like me needs
Someone like that.
Because,
Someone like that needs
Someone like me!

Has Been

Most think of a "has been" as someone once having a lucrative career or a large margin of success and are now washed up. The essence of this poem is that we find success through Christ Jesus because we've allowed Him to make us "has beens" to sin.

Sunday, October 24, 2010

He says I have been on drugs;
Turned into a thug.
The life I had was so snug
That it almost chocked the life from me.
I'd hide it under a rug
But there isn't one big enough to cover the blasphemy
Or the scars you see
From the violence I dealt
Or the bullets them other cats felt
From my gun.
Who cared that it was wrong?
It's either kill or be killed.
You can't afford to feel for the victim.
No one tricked him into coming after me.
He could've gone another way.
But then again, I didn't have a choice!
Or do I?

She claims it's all she's ever known.
She has always been grown
(at least in the mouth)
Since she was 2
Multiply that by 3 and add 4
And you get the first time she messed with a boy willingly.

(The other six times weren't her doing
So you can't count them as her choosing
To mess around.)
At least they stayed around
Longer than her father,
Gave her more attention than her mother,
Never protected her like a brother
Should;
But this ain't a family thing.
This is a caged bird singing
"You'll get all of me
But you gotta pay."
She didn't know the cost
Of tricking
Was more than she could afford
Because you can't make men your lord
And still be the Lord's…
But it's all she knew.

Now the twins Michael & Mary
Quite contrary
They've been in church
Since they were in the womb.
Their outside is righteous
But their inside is consumed
With the lust of the flesh
And the pride of life.
Everything they do is right
Cause their parents said they could do no wrong.
So they just go along,
Snubbing their peers,
Faking their tears,
Pretending to repent,

But what they do
Is sinful too
Because their righteousness
Is nasty boo.
It's like dirty rags
And that just won't do.
And these twins
Have no clue
That they're bound for Hell
Just like the other two.

If any of these lines describe you,
Or are absolutely nothing like you
I STILL got something to tell you.
I don't care what your past has been;
I don't care what your life has been;
I don't care that you're a has been;
For He has been
Wounded
For the "has been"
And had He not been
We could not be
Heirs with Him
Carrying with Him
The cross
We'd be lost
And the price He paid
Wouldn't be worth the cost.

He came to present a choice to the dealer
And show him how to hustle grace
And sling faith
Instead of rocks.

And for the trickster,
He wants to show her how to get richer
In love
By giving Him to others
And saving herself for the *only* Brother
That died for her
And her pimp too.
And the love He gives won't abuse her
Like the pimps do.
And Michael & Mary
Could be new
If they changed their self-righteous ways
And spent their days
Seeking His face
For strength to run the race
Instead of being a disgrace
To the faith and body of Christ.
You know they won't right.
But that's how we do
We either straight out sin
And don't repent again
Because there's no conviction to change
Or we go each day
Forgetting to pray
Because we spend too much time
Criticizing
And trying to hide it,
The iniquity that's inside us.
We'd rather fuss
Than confess
That we're in a mess
But that's what I had been
Before I knew He had been

Sacrificed for me
And He did it freely
And I'm a "has been"
Who have been
Made free.

"Moreover the law entered, that the offence might abound. But where sin abounded, grace did much more abound" –Romans 5:20 KJV

"But he was wounded for our transgressions, he was bruised for our iniquities: the chastisement of our peace was upon him…" –Isaiah 53:5 KJV

"But he was pierced for our rebellion, crushed for our sins. He was beaten so we could be whole. He was whipped so we could be healed." –Isaiah 53:5 NLT

He Wanted to Die

I had a friend who was tired of living the life he had, and the only solution was to die. But he didn't necessarily want to be the one to kill himself. This poem was birthed out of that situation.

Thursday, September 15, 2016
For David

He wanted to die.
But was too coward to commit suicide,
So he'd figured he'd try by enlisting help from someone else.
He was a cop himself
So suicide by cop didn't seem an option
Because he knew someone on the force would stop him,
Ignoring his pleas and policing his situation,
Turning him over to the hospital for evaluation
And he couldn't take that chance.
He would have taken pills,
Some that would instantly kill
But his gag reflex was too strong
And he figured something would go wrong
like he'd vomit instead of swallow.
He could always follow the road
That lead to the big bridge and take a leap
Into the abyss and never float again.
But he feared he'd panic and start to swim
And then where would that lead but back to the shores of his frustration.
He did not want anyone to save him so he figured
Driving into a tree would not be ideal
Because with his luck someone would be hiding
In the still of the night and would rescue him
From dying in an intentional accident.

So that's when he went to this plan
Of having God assist him in ending his life.
He knew the Lord gave and the Lord takes away.
So, he figured he could trick Him into not letting him stay in this world any longer.
All it took was one act of rebellion and he'd immediately die,
Not having to try and try again every morning that he arose with misery by his side.
It's easier to hide in the belly of a whale than to kill one's will.
It's easier to run than to stand still and see the salvation of the Lord.
It's easier to pretend that you're having the time of your life
And that it cost you so much that you can't afford to surrender
To the Lender.
The one who lent your life and your kids.
But not even they are enough for him to do what must be done.
Excuse me, he didn't run, just jogging in place but steadily moving from the direction of grace
Because he wanted to die.
What he failed to realize is that if this is his mentality, he's already dead.
He's a dead man walking whose light is not dim but diminished.
He refuses to finish what he started because carrying a cross is not ideal.
If he can't fix himself he doesn't want to be fixed.
Yet, he wants his son to behave and his daughter to remember to pray
but they are grieving the loss of their father.
They have no one in the house to be priest
So they release their anger the best way they know how.

They refuse to bow in submission because no one was intentional about showing them how.
He was too busy trying to die.
And because his thinking is so construed, He has no clue the Father's love can't be abused.
For His desire is that none shall perish.
He cherishes a relationship with all of his children and is not willing to surrender to their will.
He will wait patiently because He is longsuffering,
Longing to end your sinful suffering with compassion and grace.
It was on the cross that debt was paid so yeah, you can afford to surrender.
I know he's undeserving but so am I that's why I chose to apply the same mercy that was given to me.
And fight for the opportunity for him to make an informed decision and not miss out on God's intention
To use him to witness to other lost causes
And let them know that because of Christ they are found.
This will never happen if he doesn't stick around.
It's not the Father who will kill him, it's his disobedience that has sealed his grave.
But thanks be to God, through Christ we can be saved.
And through the redeeming power of the blood of the Lamb
He can keep the same mentality.
But this time he wants to die.
He wants to die to self and sin.
He wants to repent and return to his first love again.
He wants to be untangled from the yoke of bondage
And pay homage to the giver of life.
He wants to imitate to his du-pli-cates how to be godly
Wholeheartedly.
He doesn't want to flee grace but instead fight the enemy
And the inner me.

He wanted to die...to sin.
He wants to live again.

Conversation

Sometimes we need to just remind ourselves of who we are and who's we are. And then go believe what you say!

> Saturday, April 22, 2017
> For the "I am Beautiful Conference"

The other day I was chilling with two friends
And we started engaging in dialogue.
Or maybe it was more like a monologue since it was
Me, myself, and I having this conversation.
I came to the realization that I didn't like how this conversation was going.
See knowing a thing and doing a thing are two different things
And I started to see that this *know it all* wasn't doing a thing about it.
She knew she was fearfully and wonderfully made
Yet she clothed herself in garments of shame,
Displaying her fear of rejection and failure.
See when she compared herself to others her age
She just didn't measure up.
I wanted to tell her
Baby, there is no fear nor failure in God.
Since you know you are fearfully and wonderfully made you need to burn
Those threads of shame
And put on a spirit of praise.
Raise your hands and your head
And thank your Creator for making you!
Realize that whatever He makes is never a mistake!
Don't look at the parts but the whole because
Vanilla extract was never meant to taste good unless it was baked

In a cake or some other delicacy.
Look at the whole that each detail brings
And accept yourself as His darling.
Just acknowledge Him in all your ways and
You can spend your days
Faith-full and instead of fearful.
She seemed to be enlightened by this bit of information
But I still sensed some hesitation on her part.
So I looked deep in her heart and saw the hole there.
It was where love of self should be and even though she loved selflessly,
It was others on the receiving end.
She was always there for her friends
And would do anything for her family.
I had to get her to see that Jesus thought she was to die for.
That makes her worth loving.
And since her value is above rubies
There is absolutely nothing that can compare.
I told her to forgive herself and share all that love with herself.
Because if she didn't no one else would know how to.
Then I grabbed my things thinking the monologue was through.
But then I realized I still had to "do."
And by that, I mean I had to be.
I had to be a better edition of me.
Loving, giving, grateful, caring.
Hopeful, enduring, patient, sharing.
I had to be me.
The poet, the teacher, the friend,
The feisty, informative, short, natural me that I was created to be.
I have to find myself in Him
So He could show me, me.

Because in all honesty no one else is qualified to be.
So I thanked me for the conversation, and then proceeded to my destination:
a place in time in space where I accept me, love me, am me!

Breathe

Self-Explanatory

Sunday and Friday, November 10 and 15, 2013

Breathe in; breathe out.
No literally, breathe in; breathe out.
Is there anyone here who is not breathing?
Because, you're the only one who shouldn't be receiving
this word, simple yet true.
God has a requirement for the rest of you
who hath breath.
You inhale His glory, His weighted presence,
And you don't hesitate to receive the presents.
You take in His beauty, His grace, mercy, and love
for you love His hand...outs.
I know you shout
the victory over the enemy
not realizing the enemy is the inner me.
You NEVER exhale praise!
Bitterness and anger flow freely
along with disappointment and doubt.
What you think comes out so loosely
it's like you suffer from diarrhea of the mouth!
And the ONLY thing He requires
you say you're too tired to render
Because you don't want to surrender
a sacrifice of praise.
Praise is comely for the upright
so you must need a new wardrobe
because your rags are wack
And you're crying broke,
But who's fault is that

When all you do is choke every time
a praise is in your throat,
Asking for a mint
as if that would cure your ailment.
I'll give it to you though, because
you do know you can't serve two masters
so you Master a form of godliness
by lifting your arms
and clapping your hands.
You'll speak to man
but you won't open your mouth to God
When He gave you voice and breath to breathe.
You dance around deliverance
like native Americans once did around a fire.
You dodge change but stand in the way of blessings
All the while you're messing over God's people.
But you know what? It's all good because your financial
breakthrough is dancing too;
All around you.
And peace of mind has joined in the jig
Along with everything else you want Him to give to you.
They're within your grasp, but you'll never reach
because you won't consistently do
What He requires of thee.
God says, "Praise me!"
Praise Him with 27umbrel and dance.
Praise Him with your voice.
Praise him not out of obligation
But like it's your pleasure and choice.
Praise Him in a dance
Like this is the last chance and opportunity
You will ever have,
for it very well may be.

Praise Him for the good.
Praise Him in the bad.
Praise, happy, sad, mad, glad.
Just praise Him.
Don't let your feelings control
Your willingness to
offer God the praise He's due.
Because no matter what,
He still blessed you
To be alive.
Don't sigh when they say, "Praise the Lord."
Just inhale blessings,
and exhale praise!
Breathe in; breathe out!

Transfusion

If we haven't experienced a transfusion or dialysis, we know people who have. Therefore, we know something about the diseases that cause the need for these procedures. This poem uses real diseases to symbolize the sin sick soul and gives insight to the cure for what's ailing you.

Sunday and Monday, December 30 and 31, 2012
w/assistance from Dr. Anthony Sawyer, MD, MPH
Inspired by: Kelvin Brown Jr.

Are you washed
In the wonder working
Power of the blood?
For I know it was the
Blood that prevails,
Rescuing me from hell
Making me whole,
Renewing my soul.
Nothing but the blood
Could reach so high
And flow so low
No matter where I go.
It doesn't matter the circumstance
Nor the condition
Or even the type
For He's O Positive
Making Him the
Original universal
Blood donor
And owner of redemption.
Did I mention
That it's common practice
For Jesus to transfuse

Good news
(aka the Gospel)
Into any blood stream
By any means necessary.
It's customary
For certain illnesses to require
Dialysis
The practice
Of purifying blood
Of impurities
Like sin, guilt and shame.
That's why Christ's
Cleansing blood came
To perform dialysis on the sin sick soul.
But maybe your symptoms
Have made you a victim of
Hemophilia.
Your soul keeps bleeding
So you need Him to stop
And clot the blood.
Or maybe you seek
A donor for your
Leukemia
That's producing pride
At a rapid rate,
Making you unable to take
Correction and constructive criticism,
Producing an infection in the mind and soul.
Or maybe you suffer
From a disease your mother
Passed down like
Sickle cell anemia.
You need someone who can

Mold and make
Your abnormal shape
Into a new creature made whole.
Because right now you're stuck
In the past
And the pain lasts
For hours on end.
You could be suffering from
Lymphoma or Myeloma
Of which neither there is a cure.
But there are ways
To strengthen you.
Yes, a transfusion will do.
Where the Lord will replace
Your malice and hate
With love and grace.
He'll give beauty for ashes,
joy for pain.
He'll let praise remain,
Clothing you festively
And majestically
So that you no longer wear the
Tattered garments of heaviness.
Yes this transfusion,
Though nothing new
Will make you a new creature
Meeker in nature
And grateful for the Savior
Who saved your life
With his blood.
But one thing you must do:
For this transfusion to be a success,
You must admit you're in a mess

And desperate for a change.
I promise He'll rearrange your thinking
(if not the situation)
But your condition
Will be in remission
Never to return.
Only if you will trust
From this day forth
That His blood will never fail.
For the soul cleansing blood of the lamb
Makes all well.

Hebrews 9:13-14 KJV
13 For if the blood of bulls and of goats, and the ashes of an heifer sprinkling the unclean, sanctifieth to the purifying of the flesh:
14 How much more shall the blood of Christ, who through the eternal Spirit offered himself without spot to God, purge your conscience from dead works to serve the living God?

1 John 1:7b KJV
7 ...and the blood of Jesus Christ his Son cleanseth us from all sin.

2 Corinthians 5:17 KJV
17 Therefore if any man be in Christ, he is a new creature: old things are passed away; behold, all things are become new.

A Heart That Forgives

Mathew 6:14-15 NLT
"If you forgive those who sin against you, your heavenly Father will forgive you. But if you refuse to forgive others, your Father will not forgive your sins."

Luke 17: 3-4 NLT
"So watch yourselves! 'If another believer sins, rebuke that person; then if there is repentance, forgive. Even if that person wrongs you seven times a day and each time turns again and asks forgiveness, you must forgive.'"

Monday, December 23, 2013

I just want a heart that forgives.
You know, the type of heart that loves
Despite how I feel.
No longer a roller coaster of emotion screaming
Every time someone trips
As if that's a dip in the ride.
I've tried to do it on my own
But it was an epic fail
And I fell
because I was too emotional to catch myself and break my fall.
I just want to move on from the wrong,
Get along well enough to move on
And move on to victory;
Let this situation be history
And not one worth repeating.
I don't want to keep retreating inside myself
And finding myself engulfed with bitterness, frustration, and/or disappointment.
I want it to be a place of peace and not of memory
Where I don't have to remember everything you said to me

Or did to me
No matter how grimey.
And if anyone tries to remind me
I can recollect there was an incident
But I don't remember the details that went along with it
Because there's no room for forgiveness AND records of wrongdoing in my heart.
I want to start
Trusting again.
Not necessarily in people
But in making amends and God's ability to heal broken hearts
And bind wounds.
I know He's able to consume the sting of pain
And erase the embarrassment and shame
But I want to believe it too;
Not just know it.
I want to know that no matter who
I can forgive whether they have my best interest at heart
Or not.
I just want to do it God's way and not lean to my understanding
Of what forgiveness should be
Because honestly God forgave me,
So I'd have THE best example of what to do.
And He did so with no guarantee that I'd be more like Him
Before being less like me.
He knew in some areas I'd be worse before getting better.
Yet, He still broke every chain and fetter
So I could be free
And take advantage of every opportunity
To forgive.
So my earnest plea
Is simply

To have a heart that forgives
Consistently.

Garden Eviction

What if the conversation that Eve had in the Garden with the serpent was not their first encounter?

Saturday, January 5, 2019

Let me take a moment to collect my thoughts.
Go back to a place of mental clarity.
Free to think.
Free to be.
A mind palace of sorts
That resembles more of the original garden
Before Eve got deceived
And she and Adam got evicted.
Before the evil one tricked her.
Maybe she wanted to be deceived.
As far as we know that's the only time she visited that tree and the serpent was there.
Or maybe they'd met before
Because she was bored with "women's work"
And needed someone to talk to.
Adam had God,
Who did she have?
I mean the serpent was a patient friend
Not a patient enemy.
That's why it seems odd to us
But not odd to Eve to have a conversation
About a forbidden tree.
I mean they'd talked about everything else:
Adam's birthmark,
How he liked his veggies steamed,
How he'd name all the animals,
How he was patient and never mean.

Conversations about her husband
But never about Eve.
"Girl what about you? What do you do?"
The serpent might have said.
She was content until that question made her mad.
What did she do? Who was she?
Only designed to please her husband?
Nah, ninja, this can't be.
Discontentment set in
And her husband and God were no longer enough
Eve was woman. Female. Tough.
So maybe by the time they got to the forbidden tree,
The serpent had already planted rebellion inside of Eve.
She shares the fruit with her husband,
Not out of kindness but out of greed
Because she needed him to see
She was more than his wife; she was Eve!
The taste was sweet, the consequences bitter
Because reality set in
The serpent tricked her.
How was she so easily beguiled?
In trying to prove a point, now everything is foul.
So here I am eons later trying not to be
As easily deceived as the first woman, Eve.
Strong. Independent. Necessary.
Not an ounce of fear
Except for when a snake appears.
"A snake might get me kicked out the garden so I steer clear."
Head to my Creator who holds me dear.
Remind myself of who I am,
Not what society thinks of me.

Those types of thoughts are the serpent slithering into my psyche.
It was that serpent's opinion that trapped up Eve.
She gave him too much authority.
So I bring into captivity
Thoughts that contradict His line of thinking.
Thoughts that have me sinking
And unbelieving.
Thoughts that leave me unsatisfied
And wanting what's forbidden.
Forbidden because the consequences
You can't get rid of no matter how remorseful you are.
I flee from the tree where the serpent talks to me
And instead go to the cool of the day.
It's there I feel a gentle breeze
Can expose all of me.
Be naked and unashamed.
My Father dialogues with me
And it's there I finally meet
Adam,
My husband.
I, his helpmeet.
We stand together.
Content with our purpose
Of this I'm certain
Because he entertains me
Instead of the serpent.
Speaking like the God he loves
Provoking me to do and be
Better.
Loving all he sees
And enjoying life,
A life with me.

More than a fairy tale…
Like the picture painted for Eve.
Because this dream of mine
Within my mind
Where I have clarity
Will soon be
Reality.

I'm Just Tired

Slothfulness and fear had become my bff (best friend forever) and I was just tired of not producing what I knew lied within me; what I knew I was capable of achieving.

Friday, January 27, 2017

I'm just tired.
I'm tired of God supplying my needs
But I don't see the need to supply Him with thanks through my actions.
I keep acting like it's His reasonable service
When serving Him is what I was created for.
I'm staring at closed doors envisioning them opening
When all I have to do is open my mouth to ask
and then open my hand to turn the knob.
I have not because I asked not
and faith without works is dead.
So I'm just tired of wanting
but not enough to go get.
My mustard seed is being choked by
the weeds of doubt, fear, insecurity and even scrutiny
from myself, not even others.
My mother and brothers believe.
My sisters and aunts intercede.
My cousins expect to see.
My uncles invest in me
but yet I do just enough to get off their radar
but not enough to be effective.
I'm neglecting gifts and talents
And we know what happens when the talented
acts talentless:
They're useless

having rusted from lack of use.
It's time I change my attitude and perception
and just do!
Because truth is, I want the best too.

Today I Cried

For the parents and their families who mourn a loss due to miscarriage.

Thursday, January 25, 2018
In loving memory...

Today I cried for the little person I never met.
See, two people dear to me, though not trying,
had beget a little seed.
Though not fully developed,
apparently it was far enough along
that God saw fit to call the dear one to their heavenly home.

Today I cried for the little person I never got to see.
Two people dear to me, though not trying,
had conceived and brought forth life.
But it was not meant for that little life to stay
so the babe took flight and went back the other way
from whence they came.

Today I cried for the little one who never cried for me.
See, two people dear to me, though not trying,
unintentionally became impregnated
And purposed to do their best in spite of it all,
But that precious gift returned when it heard the Father's call.

Today I cried for baby G. Tomorrow I rejoice
Over the fact that of all the little ones, they were God's favorite choice.
Since only the pure in heart live in heaven eternally
And oh, the joy that will fill my heart when in Heaven we finally meet.

Stages

Stages came at a time in my life when I had lost a good friend to death. And a little over a month later I lost another good friend to life meaning he was alive and well, but our lives were taking us in different directions. The finality of both situations was a hard pill to swallow but by the grace of God and this poem I was able to move forward.

Saturday, April 28, 2012

Scientifically speaking there are five stages
And I know rage has to be one, because that's where I am right now
Or maybe disappointment is a more accurate word
Because I heard things you've never said
I've seen things you've never shown
It's hard to know
And not be known! You feel me?
Of course not because I am forgotten
Forsaken
Shaken from your mind and your life
This can't be right
It wasn't supposed to be this way
I wasn't supposed to grieve this way
Over the killing of a friend
But I had to end it
Because the Lord instructed me to
But it can't be you
Who I had to let go
But I guess that's part of stage one
Denial
A Trial that I must face
As long as I'm still in His grace

I know I'll be okay
But how could you say we'd be friends forever
When you never respond
You never call
You never reply
You never ask why to anything I say anymore
I can't believe you would be so inconsiderate
And indignant to the situation
As if this was the destination I chose for us.
Yes I fuss at you in anger
Because you don't even see the danger
In the situation you created
I hate that I have to go through this
But I digress
Because I'm transitioning from stage two
To three
When I try to convince you
That we can still be friends
We can make amends and make this work
I know you were a jerk but I jerk every time
I think of not having you around
I frown at the idea of not being able to call you
Bestest or even buddy
My vision is muddy and clouded by this false hope
Of us ever being as close as before
I mean there has got to be more in store
But since I'm now in stage four I know that's not true
I'll never progress
I'll never grow
I'll never show you who I was meant to be
Because you never see me
You never come around
You're never there

Did you ever even care?
Woe is me
I now see
I was alone all along
I guess that's why stage four seems so wrong so I move to stage five
Of being alive and well
I'm just swell because I know in whom I trust
And in whom I believe
I'm ready to receive all He has in store for me
And even if I must follow with a broken heart
Or an overwhelmed mind
That's still fine
Because I know it's working for my good
He told me so in His word
And I'd rather trust Him than wait on you or even for you
For you may never come,
But He has never left
And that's why stage five is where I'll remain
Accepting change
And moving from a prison to a promise
And maintain my praise
Throughout the journey.

I Cry
A Black History Poem

Monday, February 25, 2019

And still I rise
From a dream deferred
I just heard about another unarmed man who met his demise
It seems Black lives matter
But not to blacks
Between homicide and abortion, genocide has become our portion.
I wonder if this is why Harriet stole away
Leading the way
To free
Men who remain enslaved to their mentalities.
The reality is
Booker gave us industrial education
George W. Carver showed us how to make the most of what we have
DuBois gave us formal education
And Martin wanted us to be a nation
United by the content of our character and not the color of our skin
But when we fail within we go without.
Look around.
Do we as a people really know our worth?
Black girls rock
A crop top in the middle of winter
Because they want their curves to be the center of attention
And not their brains.
Black men are the G.O.A.T. when it comes to being an inmate
But they can't take criticism or corrective instruction

If it makes them look like a punk.
They'd rather kill than deal with the realities they face daily.
Emmett Till was killed for just being a normal teen
So it would seem that we would want to be unique
Embracing our identity as the kings and queens we descend from.
But we don't exercise our authority.
Rosa sat so Martin could walk so Obama could run
And when he was done we were too.
We allowed politics to come back and abuse us once more.
Looking for greater
Hoping for more
But doing nothing.
So I cry. I cry for the nation who fought so hard and gave so much
For a people who don't even know who they are any more.
I cry for the child who feels so entitled but doesn't want to work to get what they're owed.
I cry for the parent who doesn't know what to do
And where to turn to
Because the community quit parenting them.
I cry for the slaves who fought
The kids who demonstrated
The political leaders who sought social change
So we wouldn't have to sit in the back
But yet, it's still our go to spot.
I cry out to my nation of various hues
And ask us to stop.
Stop redefining right to fit our wrongs
Because doing so has caused confusion.
Stop being so caught up in self
That you can't help someone else reach their full potential.
I cry out to my little sisters

And I remind them that God made them beautiful
And unusual
And you don't have to compromise for the world to realize it.
I cry out to my little brothers
And remind them that they were created to lead
So don't leave us stranded
By choosing things that will take your life.
We need you here to help us fight social and moral injustices.
I cry out to the parents and grandparents who have gotten off their knees
Enjoying middle class
Thinking we're free at last.
We're not and if your prayers cease
Who will intercede for this lost generation.
I cry out to my Creator
Thank Him for being so faithful
And then ask Him not to let me take His favor for granted.
Because whether a colored negro or a black African American
You're definitely someone special
Not just on the third Monday of January
Or the 28 days of this month
But everyday.
But if we don't join together
And value what we have
And who we are
We'll think we're gaining leaps and bounds
When reality is we're becoming extinct.
So look to your left.
And look to your right.
Look within and let all 3 of those people
Be your reason
For making a deferred dream reality.

A Mother's Day Tribute

In honor of my mother and all mothers who live, give, and sacrifice willingly and lovingly.

Saturday, May 10, 2015

Mom,

I am because you are.
I am more than your "mini me"
I am destiny fulfilled.
You had a choice and
You chose to let live
And not kill
And for that I am grateful.
Your blood flows through my veins
And it's something I should not be ashamed to admit.
I may or may not be your spitting image
But my DNA is evidence that I am an extension of you.
Your labor of love to keep a roof over my head
Clothes on my back
Food on the table
Supplies for my education
Is appreciated today and always.
For every extra hour you worked
To make ends meet
For every time I was rewarded and given a treat
Looked in the crowd and you were standing there
Even if I was just a bench warmer
And would never receive academic recognition
You recognized me as a winner
And for that I'm grateful.
I may not say it often,
And it seems like I take you for granted
And sometimes you would be right.
I do.
But when I reflect and look back

I find myself doing some of the same things you do
Because I am an imitator and I do what you do.
Out of obedience, I do what you say.
I find myself talking to God daily because daily you called to Him for help.
I am confident because you were confident that I would be someone and not another statistic.
I don't want you to feel like you missed it – the mark.
In some areas you may have
But over all I'm not a bad person
So when you look at the sum of your efforts
And not the individual deductions
You see I'm still functioning well in society.
I don't want you to think my bad choices are a direct result of how you raised me
Because I'm still my own person.
But because you gave me a good start
I know within my heart
That I'm better than any wrong decision
And by the grace of God
I can live up to the vision.
Yes, I am your daughter or son
Who you've molded like clay
And I can become everything you say
So, continue to speak well over me.
Train me to be the best me I can be.
I know it's easier said than done
But I need you to trust
That God has given you what you need
I mean after all,
He did give you me.
And if He can trust you with so delicate of a gift
I can continue to trust you to lift my spirits
And invest your time in seeing me flourish.
Because you're a reflection of
the Heavenly Father's love for me.
I want to continue to see Him in your interactions with me.

I'm not expecting perfection
Just a mother who's trusting the Father to guide her along the way.
I guess I said all this just to say.
I love you Mom.
And not just on Mother's Day.

Dear Dad

In honor of my father and all fathers; those who plant the seed, those who water, and those who look lovingly as God yields the increase.

Saturday, June 18, 2016

Dear Dad,
    I want you to know I'm not mad.
I'm actually glad to be able to identify with you.
A good father always makes you want to.
I looked in the dictionary
and it was made apparent to me
that a father is not just who you are;
it's what you do!
For you see Father is a noun and verb too
It's a man in relation to his natural child
Whether naturally born or we just naturally get along
Like the Father to His son.
It's a man who gives care and protection to someone
And from day one you've had me on your mind.
I know from time to time I wasn't dealing with you
Or feeling the way you'd interact with me.
Often times we'd disagree but that was
Primarily because I didn't understand,
You're not just a man but with my birth you became father.
You are my source; where I originate from.
When you impregnated my mother
So that I could become
You gave me my identity: X or Y.
I asked her why.
She said Fathers give
Like God gave.
No matter who he is, he will always show you Christ.
Either a true view or a distorted image.
I know He's not finished with you

Just like you aren't finished with me.
But I want to encourage you to not be distracted by what you see.
TV will have you believe that there's no need for you because
The "I'm every woman" can be you.
But that's not true.
Don't believe the lie that we don't need you to provide.
We need your resources and your time.
And please know that DNA doesn't mean we'll do *always* do things the same way.
If anything, encourage me to do better
So I can be in a better position to look out for you.
Honestly, I want to.
And one last thing before I go.
Make sure your brothers, uncles, nephews, cousins, and homies know
This letter is for them too.
I'm thankful for any male whom father is more than an identity, it's what he does.
He Fathers us out of love.
Always,
Your Child

I'm a Raisin (Raising)

My Pastor preached about us being raisins: dried up grapes that YET have purpose! This poem goes through the details of a horrific car accident I had Tuesday, Aug 30, 2011 and my response to the accident.

                Tuesday, November 15, 2011

(Singing) We bring a sacrifice of praise, into the house of the Lord. We bring a sacrifice of praise, into the house of the Lord. And we offer up to you, the sacrifices of thanksgiving. And we offer up to you the sacrifices of praise.

Oh I do huh? I bring a sacrifice of praise?
Don't get me wrong, I'm praising,
Because you can see I'm raising my hands…
But I question whether it's truly a sacrifice
See He spared my life
So I count it a privilege and an honor
To lift my hands
And lift my voice
It's a choice that I don't take likely
It frightened me to open my eyes
And see that I'm headed straight for the trailer
Of an 18-wheeler
I still feel the pain in my ankle
And even for that I'm grateful because
I realize that means I'm not paralyzed from the waist down
I could walk around with a frown
For I was on the move and constantly on the go
Now my life is moving so much slower than before
I want more and more to be able to drive
And get around as I did pre-accident
But that's not meant to be…at least not right now.
I don't know how my bills will be paid
Considering there's no way for me to go to work

I used to jerk in my sleep I guess subconsciously
Reliving the accident
That's more than a dent on the driver side of my car
I had to be cut out because I couldn't get out
Without assistance
No it wasn't a long distance from the job to my home
But somehow I still zoned out
And now the only way out of this car
Is by the grace of God
I called His name and while I waited for help
I sang His praises
"Yes Jesus loves me" just kept stirring in my soul
He had to love me because He took control
And brought me out with minimal damage
The story my car tells is that I should be dead
But instead He brought me out.
So the situation dictates that I could frown...
I mean life's not like it was before
I'm more like a grape drying in the sun
But that's why I smile because this
Dried grape is now a raisin.
That's right...I'm a Raisin,
Raising my hands in adoration
Grateful that my situation
Made me and didn't take me out
That right there is enough to shout about
No I can't dance right now
But I have no problems with my voice
So I keep His praise in my mouth continuously
For He so graciously kept me around.
I'm still sound in mind,
And He played a major part in that too
For He used lively stones
To pray me through
That's the process a raisin goes through.
That's right...I'm a Raisin,
Raising my hands in adoration

Grateful that my situation
Made me and didn't take me out
He filled me even the more with His Spirit
He didn't take the anointing away
But made it greater
He's such a wonderful Savior!
For there's no way He'd spare my life
And let me lose my soul.
He kept me here so I could dry and be a raisin
That's right…I'm a Raisin,
Raising my hands in adoration
Grateful that my situation
Made me and didn't take me out
And now I know there's a plan
At first I didn't understand
But then again who really knows the mind of God
That's why I go hard
Right in my chair, and all by myself
Because I could have lost myself
And never been found in Him
But I am, because He chose to turn me into a raisin.
Something still edible
That can sweeten cereal
And endures longer than any grape ever could
Now I would continue
But someone else is on after me
I just wanted you to see that for me
Praising is not a sacrifice
But a reasonable service that I render
To a life saving God
Who's made me into a raisin.
That's right…I'm a Raisin,
Raising my hands in adoration
Grateful that my situation
Made me and didn't take me out
And that right there is enough to shout about!
I'M A RAISIN!

Bonus:
Dearest Pastor

Saturday, April 7, 2018

Dearest Pastor Sawyer,

You have been an intricate part of my life even before Mt. Zion. I looked forward to every Sunday you had to preach when we were still at the Star. It wasn't about how quick you were but how much depth you put into a short amount of time. But instead of rewinding I shall fast forward to '99 when you took the responsibility of founding a church. I can about guarantee you understood the workload but probably didn't understand just how much work would have to go into this ministry. How much sacrifice and endurance would be necessary to complete the task at hand. Man, I bet (but not really because I'm saved) oftentimes you wanted to quit, pass the torch before you had finished the assignment at hand. I believe in your mind you often ran away from responsibility. Yet, here we are 19 years later praising you for your faithfulness and accountability. You never wavered. Maybe that isn't the right word; steadfast is probably better. You remained steadfast. You never physically walked away from it all. For that, I am glad.

See, it takes a lot to do what you do. I'm not talking about just preaching but teaching people how to love according to God's word and then have to demonstrate it when you leave the pulpit. Most people don't get how you have to give an account for how you Pastor. We just fuss and complain about change not realizing if you stay the same after God told you to change He'd get you. And I'm sorry but they say only the insane do the same thing twice expecting different results. I'm glad that's not you. Now don't get it twisted, foundational things should always remain in tact: prayer, Bible studying, fasting are not compromise-able if we want to make it in any day and time. Yeah, I made up a word just like you; it worked too because I know you knew what I meant.

I'm glad God sent you to pastor me. I'm sure every member here agrees. It's not the sermons although they are rhema and life to the soul. It's not the constant sowing although where there's no planting seeds will not grow. It's the character and integrity displayed when no one knows how you really think or feel. It's the fact you trust God even when you can't feel him near. It's the vulnerability you share to give us the opportunity to keep you accountable to your work and ministry. It's not that you're the perfect man it's the fact that you mark the one who is. You give and give, enduring pain, shame, disappointment just like Christ did. Good pastors do.

So I guess I just want to take the time to encourage you. I know sometimes your heart is hurting, head held down by grief. I know sometimes the burden is heavy and you just want a little relief. I know sometimes the pain seems unbearable and you just can't stop the flow of tears. I know sometimes you have no clue and you can't get a handle on your fears. I know sometimes it's just overwhelming, frustrating, and maybe disappointing too. But Pastor, no matter the feeling or emotion, just remember this saying applies to you: "It's not in a feeling, it's in a knowing." So know that He that hath begun a good work, will perform it until the day of Christ. He giveth strength to the faint and to them that have no might. He chose you from the foundation of the world. He'll keep you from falling no matter what the Enemy may hurl in your direction. He'll protect you in the midst of the storm. No good thing does he withhold from them that walk upright. Just grab onto hope, don't let it go; squeeze it and hold on tight. Know that sometimes weeping does endure for the night. But joy comes with the morning light. And know at the end of every day, you'll be alright. For His grace is sufficient for thee. It's really all you need. Every promise in the book belongs to you; there's no need to speed through life. For the race is given to the one who endures not necessarily the first to arrive. You're doing a good job Pastor. Keep it up! The church will thrive.

    And before I go, I wanted you know, I honor and respect you, sir. I pray for you daily and I do my best to serve. And because I can't carry your cross, like you can't carry mine, I intercede for you and take this time to let you know you're not in this alone, and God will give you the strength to carry on. Happy Anniversary Pastor!

                        Sincerely,
                        SeLisa